You

In A Book!

Writing Your Story Through Journaling

MIKI BENNETT

Copyright ©2019 by Miki Bennett

ISBN-13: 978-0-9988481-6-7

WannaDo Publishing, LLC, Charleston, South Carolina

*This book is dedicated to everyone who
loves to stretch their imaginations!*

Buzzword: Journaling!

Journaling! These days it seems like everywhere I look I see so much about writing your thoughts on paper: social media posts, "how to" blogs, videos and more. People are sharing their love for keeping a journal or diary more than ever before. I think it is great! I love that journals are finding more popularity among everyone as people realize the importance of how a blank book can change their world.

People have been keeping diaries or journals for centuries. As a matter of fact, many personal journals discovered from our ancestors have given us a glimpse into the past from how people worked, ate, spent their days, etc. They have also provided accounts of historical events that have helped us piece history together. But journaling has become so much more in today's world though bits and pieces still remain the same.

There are so many terrific reasons for writing down your thoughts.
* It's a great way to capture memories! In time, reading your older journals is so much fun and eye opening. You can't help but

reminisce about moments in your life that make you "You".

* Taking time to write your thoughts down can help you when you need to solve a problem. Reading the ideas you've written and giving them more thought, maybe even making more notes, can help you find the answers you are seeking.

* It can help you establish your future dreams and goals then go on to accomplishing them. You can also keep track of your progress as you work each day to reach those dreams of yours.

* You'll have a record of your personal growth. Over time, by consistently writing in your journal, you will be able to see how you have improved in all areas of your life.

This is just a smidgen of the things your own personal journal can offer you. My hope is that this journal will help you with all the above plus bring out your creative side when it comes to a blank book and writing your thoughts.

A Blast From The Past

Recently I came across a plastic box full of notebooks. It puzzled me at first because I was sure I knew where all my books and papers were – on a shelf or filed away! But as I lifted the lid, a huge smile crossed my face. The box held years worth of my personal journals. Books and papers from the time I was a little girl till only a few years ago. I had forgotten I put them in the box for storage.

I have kept journals and planners since I could write. As a young girl I thought there was something magical about a book completely devoid of writing. When others saw blank pieces of paper, I saw loads of possibilities. At that time in my life these books were called "diaries". I even had one that had a lock on it with a special key to keep prying eyes away! Sadly, it was lost along the way as I grew up but I remember the happiness it brought into my life.

As a teenager, I kept a journal but also added a spiral notebook to my daily collection that would later become my planner. Both of my parents were entrepreneurs and I watched them make daily, weekly and monthly to-do lists in notebooks while consulting a big calendar on the wall for planning. That was their method of staying organized and I was determined to do the same. My journal stayed safely at home but my notebook/planner went everywhere with me. And that is how it is to this day.

After exploring the different books in the box, I found one of the oldest of the bunch and read a few entries. As I read I could recall a time when life was simpler. I had written about my school, playing with friends outside till the streetlights came on, building forts in the woods and more. In another journal I wrote about high school clubs I had joined, the proms I went to and high school graduation. From there another book documented my journey into becoming a wife and then a mother. As I read entry after entry I was so glad that I had kept a record of my memories, thoughts and opinions over the years.

So why am I teaching about journaling?

You can tell by now that I love the journaling process so this could be a long story but I'll try to condense it as best as I can.

I've LOVED – really loved – blank books, papers, pens, notebooks, planners and more since I was a young girl. When I would go shopping with my parents, they could find me in the office supply section of the store instead of the toy aisle. In my world, blank books were treasures that I loved to fill up with memorabilia, papers I found, color in them and yes write my deepest thoughts. I collected these blank books and would get excited as one book filled and I was able to move on to the next.

Each of those journals show a progression in my life from a child to a young adult to the woman I've become now. The words I've written have been everything from joy to sadness and back again, like a rollercoaster. There are so many life lessons in the pages and words that when I feel like I need a friend to talk to, I can read past journal entries and feel comforted.

You In A Book!

Though I have filled many a book, there are still so many unanswered questions. Life is always changing with new experiences and learning adventures. Until recently I wrote my daily thoughts but then I started exploring questions that I had never asked myself. Some of them were hard and made me think deep, at times taking more than a day to answer. Other questions were fun and helped me remember the parts of myself that I had neglected or filed away in my mind for one reason or another.

I began to answer some questions or what I call "Journal Prompts" in my journal. That's when I decided it was time to put a book together where I could help others. People could discover the fun of writing their thoughts, taking them on a journey of self-discovery by answering some questions, and maybe dip into a bit of creativity while they were writing. The book I'm talking about is the one you hold in your hands.

How To Journal

Now you might wonder why there is a section titled "How To Journal". All you have to do is write in a blank book, right? Well, that is part of it but there is so much more you can add to your journaling experience that can make it even more fun and satisfying. Like I said before, I only wrote my thoughts when I first began but, as I got older and let my imagination step outside of the box, I discovered many ways that you can bring more life to your journal than mere written words.

I really started putting my own spin on my daily writing when I began using colored pens. I am a girl who is obsessed with color – the brighter the better! I color coded entries and doodled in the margins. I was having so much fun and the different colors dotting the pages made me smile. But then I thought what fun it would be to add paper clippings, ticket stubs, receipts, etc., to my book. I let my creativity roam. Some days it was just words and others it was a full page of color, pictures, drawings and more. Before long I had thick journals instead of the thin notebooks I was used to.

Now I want to give you several suggestions on different ways you can journal in the following pages. The key to remember is that THIS IS YOUR BOOK! Use whatever techniques you like. This is your story – your style – your vibe. Isn't that cool? It can be minimalistic or have so much color it looks like it went to a paintball park! It can be thin and neat or so thick that you need a rubber band to keep it together. The sky is the limit! Let your creativity roam!

1. *Just write your thoughts*

This is the minimalist approach to journaling. I say that with love because I did this for many years. Write your thoughts. Write about your day. Write about a business idea you have. Write about your family vacation. Just write. I would encourage you to pick your favorite writing pen or pencil. That way each time you make an entry it makes the process more special for you.

2. *A touch of color*

So where are my people that love color? I love using different colors in all my journals and planners. For me it makes the book look happy which in turn makes me smile. But I also like the way it challenges me to use color in creative ways while writing. This might be using a certain color on particular days. It could mean writing your title in one color, the entry in another and a quote in yet another color.

Also with color, choose different pens or pencils. I love markers! And even if the writing bleeds from one side to the next, I feel that it just gives my journal more character. I'm not about the journal being perfect but being uniquely all mine.

3. Add Some Pictures

Now this can be so much fun! Have you ever thought of adding a picture to your journal entry? I adore this idea because you will have a photo right beside the very thing you are writing about. It brings this particular entry to life! Even if you are writing about something from a journal prompt, there are pictures you can print from your own stash of photos or something off the internet (for personal use only please) that can make that entry even more special.

4. Stickers Everywhere

Did I also say that I love stickers? They are the best! I've used stickers in many different ways in my journals and planners. They have decorated the edges of the pages. I've used square box stickers and written about a special moment in each box. Then I might doodle around them. You can get stickers just about everywhere, order them online or make your own with some sticker paper, a printer and pictures. I have my own very large stash of stickers that I love and if I happen to visit Etsy.com I'm in trouble! There are hundreds of stores on the website that make some of the cutest stickers that are both useful and fun to add a little spice to your journal.

5. Doodle, Doodle, Doodle

I know you like to doodle! Doesn't everyone? You know those squiggly marks that you draw, connecting the lines to form different shapes and objects. You usually doodle when you are thinking or trying to relax. I know sometimes I find myself doodling when I'm on the phone chatting with someone. But I also have a sketchbook filled with doodles or Zentangles as I like to call them. In a journal they can add a touch of whimsy around your writing entry. And if you want to take it a step further, color in your doodle!

6. Extra special touches

There are little special touches that you can add to your journal that can make it even more unique to you. You can use Washi Tape around the edges of the page for a polished or colorful look. You can add ribbon, glitter, pressed flowers, yarn, bookmarks and more. There are so many little things you can include among the pages of your journal. The only limit here is your imagination.

7. Word(s) of the day

How about adding a word of the day? Adding a special word that describes your day is a very individual thing. It could be a word that describes your writing, a vocabulary word you want to learn and incorporate into everyday use, a value that is important to your life and more. Some people like to add quotes each day or a spiritual scripture or text. Words like this add special meaning to your journal.

Isn't this awesome? Your journal can become whatever you want it to be. All you have to do is relax, tap into your imagination and let it soar!

Journal Prompts

Now that we know how to journal are you ready for some journal prompts? Most people like to write about their day but I encourage you to explore these prompts. They are perfect when you have that day where you want to explore a particular subject deeper or add to your writing skills. Just pick your category then look for the prompt that speaks to you. You'll know what you want to write about as soon as you see the prompt. And don't censor yourself. Write your thoughts. Write your opinions. Write your ideas. This is your book. <u>This is "You" in a book!</u>

All About You

* What skills do you have that others don't?
* What is your current job? Do you like it?
* Who is your biggest inspiration and why?
* What inspires you right now?
* What makes you laugh?
* How have you changed in the last five years?
* If you could travel to any destination in the world, where would it be and why?
* What surprises you the most about your life right now?
* What are your unique gifts and talents?
* If you could do something all over again differently, what would it be?
* What's your favorite personality trait?
* What's a funny story that makes you laugh every time you hear it?

Family Matters

* Are you an only child or do you have siblings?
* What was your favorite family vacation?
* How do you, along with your family, celebrate each other?
* Do you eat dinners together? Why or why not?
* How satisfied are you with your social life?
* How do you feel about having children?
* Call a family member today then write about your talk.
* Who in your family are you the closest to? Why?
* Does your family have big reunions each year to catch up and see each other?
* Is there a family member that made you cry? What happened?
* Is there a family member you are jealous of? If so, why?
* Does your family encourage you as you pursue your dreams?

Go For the Goal

* What does your dream life look like?
* Where do you see yourself in six months? A year? Five years? Ten years?
* What does happiness mean to you?
* If you knew you couldn't fail what would you do?
* Do you use a visualization exercise each day, seeing yourself succeeding at your goals?
* List three things you know would help you move closer to your goals.
* Write all the things you learned from doing things the "hard" way. How can you make things easier?
* What words move and inspire you?
* Write about your number one goal and why it is most important right now.
* Make a list of goals you have already accomplished.
* Do you have a vision board to be able to see your goals each day?
* Do you belong to any groups that help you toward achieving your goals?

Getting Personal

* Are you happy with your life right now?
* What is one thing you are good at?
* What is your biggest fear?
* Do you feel successful in your life?
* Are you comfortable with your finances?
* What does your ideal day look like?
* What has been bothering you lately?
* How do you feel about your current relationship status?
* What do you need to do to make more time for yourself?
* What is something that you wished for that came true?
* What is one thing you look forward to everyday?
* Who do you trust most right now and why?

Getting Healthy

* If you are feeling low how do you cheer yourself up?
* How do you handle stressful situations?
* Do you have a self-care routine?
* What are your go to healthy foods?
* What is your favorite exercise routine?
* Do you like to meditate?
* How are you feeling right now?
* What would your health look like at its best? What would you be doing every day?
* List three things you want to change about your health.
* What are five ways you can relax?
* What do you need to work on most for your health?
* Write a thank-you letter to your body for all that it can do.

You Gotta Have Friends

* Who is your best friend? Why?
* What do you and your friends like to do?
* Who are your three closest friends and why?
* Would you go on a "friends only" travel vacation?
* Do you feel comfortable sharing your most personal secrets with your friends?
* How do you feel about gossip?
* How would you like your closest friends to describe you?
* Write about a time when you helped a friend in need.
* What does good communication look like to you in a friendship?
* What do you feel is unforgiveable in a friendship?
* Do you prefer a small or large circle of friends?
* What makes you a good friend?

Self Confidence

* Are you pushing yourself to your highest potential?
* What are ten positive things about your life?
* If you could give your younger self some advice what would it be?
* What are ten things you love about yourself?
* What compliment do people give you the most?
* What kind of person do you want to be?
* How can you live your life more passionately?
* Why are you worth knowing?
* When do you feel most confident?
* Give yourself a compliment.
* What is your proudest moment?
* What would make your teenage self proud of the person you have become?

What About Gratitude

* What are you grateful for today?
* How has gratitude changed your life?
* What can you do to improve your feelings of gratitude?
* Who do you look up to and why?
* What is the nicest thing someone has ever said to you?
* What book have you read that you are grateful for?
* What is something you take for granted?
* What is something you are grateful for out in nature?
* What is something that you are grateful for that helps you to relax?
* What are you grateful for about your home?
* What is a favorite quote or saying that makes you happy?
* Look at your hands. Write something positive about them.

Getting Un-Stuck

* What do you need more of in your life?
* What do you need to let go of?
* What do you need to get off your chest today?
* What advice should you give yourself?
* How can you simplify your life in small ways?
* What activities make you the happiest?
* What could you do today to bring a smile to your face?
* Make a list of things you are good at and choose one to do. Afterwards write about your experience.
* What do you want more of in your life? How can you get that?
* What is one thing you accomplished and how did you do it? How could you use those same techniques to complete something you are working on now?
* Who can you turn to for solid, good advice?
* Write any regrets you have and let them go in order to move on.

Your Favorites

* What was your favorite toy as a child?
* What is your favorite book?
* What is your favorite animal?
* What is your favorite childhood memory?
* What is your favorite school memory?
* What is your favorite holiday?
* What is your favorite meal?
* What are the favorite things about your job?
* What is your favorite thing that makes life easier for you?
* What is your favorite thing you use every single day?
* What is your favorite song?
* What is your favorite kind of weather?

Now you have the prompts for those times when you want to explore something else besides your day to day living. Some of the questions seem like "Yes" or "No" answers but they are much more than that. Dig deep when answering the prompt and think about all aspects of the question or statement. I bet you will write more on the subject than you think.

Most of all have fun! This is YOUR book! I have given you some suggestions on how to personalize it but it is all up to you. I cannot wait to hear about your journey or see pictures of your journal creations.

Congratulations!
You created a book about
You!

I hope you've enjoyed this journal as much as I did as I created it. As you can see, I'm passionate about journaling (and planning too!). I love journal prompts that help you think outside the norm, but then I love writing about what is going on currently in my life. The little extras I wrote about earlier let me be creative around the written word and it is something I encourage everyone to do.

So whether you keep it simple or go all out like I do sometimes, these journals of yours are as precious as you are. Enjoy them and hopefully pass the "journaling" bug on to friends and family.

For more journal prompts, please visit my website – www.mikibennett.com – every Monday. I post new questions to help you on your journaling journey. Plus, I plan to offer new journals in the future with new covers and new prompts. I'll be announcing them on my website and in my monthly newsletter!

Have Fun!
Miki

Books by Miki Bennett

"The Florida Keys Novels"

The Keys to Love

Forever in the Keys

Run Away to the Keys

Back to the Keys

A Wedding in the Keys

"Camping in High Heels" Series

Camping in High Heels

Camping in High Heels: Las Vegas

Camping in High Heels: California

Camping in High Heels: Yellowstone

Coming Soon:

Camping in High Heels: Niagara Falls

Camping in High Heels: Brandon

About The Author

Miki Bennett is the best-selling author of two novel series: *The Florida Keys Novels* and *Camping in High Heels* series. She has won numerous awards for her novels and artwork.

Miki is an avid writer, loves to journal and stay organized with planning books. She loves tapping into her creativity by trying new crafts but also loves to crochet and paint. Her "happy place" is the beach where she spends as much time as possible. She lives in Charleston, South Carolina with her husband, Jeff and little dog, Emma.

67807418R00085